OF

RICA

All rights reserved. Published in the United States by Doubleday, an imprint
of Random House Children's Books, a division of Penguin Random House LLC, New York.

Doubleday and the colophon are registered trademarks of Penguin Random House LLC.

Visit us on the Web! rhcbooks.com

Educators and librarians, for a variety of teaching tools, visit us at RHTeachersLibrarians.com

Library of Congress Cataloging-in-Publication Data
Names: Gilland, Åsa, author, illustrator.
Title: Welcome to Arizona / by Åsa Gilland.
Description: First edition. | New York : Doubleday, [2021] | Audience: Ages 3–7 |
Summary: "An illustrated introduction to the state of Arizona" —Provided by publisher.
Identifiers: LCCN 2020009804 (print) | LCCN 2020009805 (ebook)
ISBN 978-0-593-17821-8 (hardcover) | ISBN 978-0-593-17822-5 (ebook)
Subjects: LCSH: Arizona—Description and travel—Juvenile literature. | Arizona—Juvenile literature.
Classification: LCC F811.3 .G55 2021 (print) | LCC F811.3 (ebook) | DDC 917.91—dc23

MANUFACTURED IN CHINA
10 9 8 7 6 5 4 3 2 1
First Edition

WELCOME to ARIZONA

illustrated by Åsa Gilland

Doubleday Books for Young Readers

WELCOME to ARIZONA!
WE'RE GLAD YOU'RE HERE!

ALASKA

WASHINGTON
OREGON
MONTANA
IDAHO
WYOMING
NORTH DAKOTA
SOUTH DAKOTA
MINNESOTA
WISCONSIN
MICHIGAN
NEW YORK
CALIFORNIA
NEVADA
UTAH
COLORADO
NEBRASKA
IOWA
ILLINOIS
INDIANA
OHIO
PENNSYLVANIA
WEST VIRGINIA
VIRGINIA
KANSAS
MISSOURI
KENTUCKY
NORTH CAROLINA
NEW MEXICO
PHOENIX
ARIZONA
OKLAHOMA
ARKANSAS
TENNESSEE
SOUTH CAROLINA
GEORGIA
MISSISSIPPI
ALABAMA
HAWAII
TEXAS
LOUISIANA
FLORIDA

Capital city: Phoenix
State nickname: The Grand Canyon State
State motto: "Ditat Deus" ("God Enriches")

ARIZONA

ARIZONA

Nature is extra beautiful in Arizona, with deserts, mountains, canyons, and amazing rock formations. Where would you like to go first?

KINGMAN

BULLHEAD CITY

LAKE HAVASU CITY

YUMA

SAN LUIS

SAGUARO
CACTUS BLOSSOM

Don't get too close to Arizona's state flower!
The saguaro cactus blossom grows on a plant with
sharp stickers. A cactus can live in the hot, dry
Sonoran Desert by saving water inside its trunk.

CACTUS
WREN

You'll also find Arizona's state bird, the cactus wren, in the desert. This clever bird makes its nest in cactus plants, where the pointy stickers keep its eggs safe from other animals.

Arizona's state mammal, the ringtailed cat, is not a cat!
It is a member of the raccoon family. It mostly sleeps
during the day and is awake at night. Its big eyes help
it see in the dark.

RINGTAILED CAT

THE MOST DELICIOUS INSECTS

There were once much bigger creatures here: dinosaurs!

CHINDESAURUS

SONORASAURUS

Giants such as Dilophosaurus, Sarahsaurus, Sonorasaurus, and Chindesaurus roamed the land—maybe even where you're standing right now! ROAR!

DILOPHOSAURUS

SARAHSAURUS

Arizona is home to many Native American people, including the Navajo, Tohono O'odham, Apache, Hopi, and Pueblo nations.

The Navajo are also called the Diné. They are famous for making beautiful arts and crafts, such as silver and turquoise jewelry, woven rugs, baskets, and pottery.

People from around the world come to Arizona to see the Grand Canyon. This long, deep valley was formed over millions of years, as the Colorado River carved through the rock.

Some of the amazing animals that live here are bighorn sheep, mountain lions, rattlesnakes, and Gila monsters.

MONUMENT VALLEY

is another beautiful place to visit. Here you'll see huge sandstone rocks that stick up out of the desert. Two of them look like mittens with pointy thumbs!

From spicy snacks to yummy breads,
Arizona has a lot of delicious food.

CHIMICHANGAS

CHEESE CRISP

SONORAN HOT DOG

TOSTADAS

POSOLE

ENCHILADAS

ARIZONA HOT SAUCE

FRY BREAD

MARRANITOS

SOPAPILLAS

TACOS

SOPAPILLAS

BURRITOS

HONEY

TAMALES

WHICH one is your FAVORITE?

An interesting state like Arizona has a lot of unusual things to see if you're out for a drive:

597

FOUR CORNERS

There's one place in the United States where you can stand in four states at once! The borders of Arizona, Colorado, Utah, and New Mexico all meet at Four Corners.

LONDON BRIDGE

This bridge has come a *long* way! In 1968, it was bought by a man who had it shipped from London, England, to Arizona, piece by piece!

JACK RABBIT TRADING POST

Be sure not to zoom past the large billboard on Historic Route 66 that says HERE IT IS. If you do, you'll miss a giant rabbit statue you can sit on!

If you love Arizona, then you're an Arizona kid!
And Arizona kids are the best!

Yá'át'ééh!

¡HoLA!

UNITED STATES AME